EAGLE or CHICKEN

> *Winners are people who never give up.*

EGON FALK

Copyright © Egon Falk 2022
Published by BUOY MEDIA LLC
https://www.buoy-media.com

No part of this book may be reproduced, scanned, or distributed in any printed or electronic form without permission from the author.

The Author holds exclusive rights to this work. Unauthorized duplication is prohibited.
All rights reserved.

Cover design by Juan Villar Padron
https://www.juanjpadron.com

Photo credit to Lee Bailey
http://leebaileyphotography.com/

Special thanks to my editor Janell Parque
http://janellparque.blogspot.com/

Meeting Hannah, my beloved wife, in August 1969 changed the course of my entire life.

Without her, it would not have been possible for me to write this book.

My life and ministry have been shaped in partnership with Hannah.

It has not always been a walk in the park, and the harsh realities of life have sometimes poured over us like a mighty storm. In these crises, you, Hannah, have been like a diamond, only becoming more beautiful as it is cut and polished.

This process can be, and often is, very painful, but in this hidden suffering, the truth which glorifies God and blesses men is formed.

It's no secret, and I have no reservations about shouting around the whole world that you, Hannah, are the hidden, strong, and noble character in my life. Without you, my ministry would be impossible and my life so poor.

Hannah, you are like an eagle that spreads its wings and lets itself be carried by the strong but invisible winds. Together, we will soar higher and higher on the wind of the Holy Spirit and reach the goal of our lives — Tanzania must be saved and transformed.

Hannah, you are not a gossiping sparrow but a true eagle whose life is an example for others.
Arusha, Tanzania, February 1, 2022.

Dr. Egon Falk

Contents

Preface   vii

1. Character Development   1
2. How Should We Be?   7
3. Motivation   10
4. We Must Learn To Lead Ourselves Before We Can Lead Others   21
5. Character Traits And Leadership   28
6. The Right Attitude Is Mandatory   32
7. The 7 Deadly Sins   44
8. 12 Foundations Of Quality Character   51
9. 44 Quality Traits Everyone Should Develop   54
10. 60 Traits That Characterize Jesus   57
11. Authenticity Is Worth As Much As Gold   59
12. 10 Rules That Lead To Miraculous Character Development   68

Help make a difference   73
About the Author   77

Preface

You are what you are today because of the decisions you made yesterday. Your decisions today determine your day tomorrow and the rest of your future.

You decide for yourself whether you want to be an ordinary and mediocre human being, like a little chicken who walks around and only scratches the ground around his feet, is nearsighted and does not think of the future, and only moves in his own small and limited circle, to find just enough food for himself.

The most important thing is not where you come from. Never use your past as an excuse for not being able to accomplish something great in your life.

Also, do not use your background in a poor or broken family as an excuse. The best thing you can do is to forget all your "excuses" as quickly as possible and focus on the most important thing — your future since this is where you will spend the rest of your life.

Don't let things that you cannot do overshadow the things that you can do. Never have contempt for the minuscule beginning and remember that it is more important to "begin" than never to get started.

My challenge to you is — DO NOT POSTPONE THE MOST IMPORTANT THINGS IN LIFE. The biggest threat to the future is indifference. Get up, do something about your circumstances and do it now. If you do not climb the mountain, your problem, or obstacle, you will never see the wonderful view of the valley.

You need to know where you want to go in life. There is no favorable wind for him who does not

Preface

know where he wants to go. In your life's journey, you will be drifting instead of sailing.

Do not be afraid to fail, for no one who is faithful can fail. You must be willing to take a chance, a risk. To win in life without risk is the same as triumphing without victory.

Do something good for yourself by being available to others and their needs. Many people are waiting for you and in need of your love and help. When you give to others and are outgoing, you will find happiness yourself.

Remember that there is always a pleasant scent on the hand that gives out roses. Distribute many roses to as many people as possible. Remember, most people need more love than they deserve.

The power that enables you to believe is the same power that enables you to be changed and renewed.

ALWAYS DO YOUR BEST AND DO IT WHOLEHEARTEDLY. IT WILL MAKE YOU A HERO.

Preface

Isaiah 40:31 "...but those who hope in the Lord will renew their strength. They will soar on wings like eagles; they will run and not grow weary; they will walk and not be faint."

Psalms 103:5 "[THE LORD] SATISFIES YOUR DESIRES WITH GOOD THINGS SO THAT YOUR YOUTH IS RENEWED LIKE THE EAGLE'S."

Become an eagle, who, with power and glory, spreads his wings and is carried by the Spirit of God high above the petty things of life. Then you become a help and blessing to your fellow human beings, as well as a worthy representative of the King of Kings, Jesus Christ, your Savior and Lord.

Sir Winston Churchill once said the following, very powerful and true words: "WHEN THE EAGLES ARE SILENT, THE PARROTS BEGIN TO JABBER."

Dr. Egon Falk

Character Development

WE NEED, more than ever, to develop God-given character traits in our lives.

Character traits like RIGHTEOUSNESS, HONESTY, and COURAGE are harder and harder to find.

There is only one true source of these character traits, and they are found only in a personal fellowship with Jesus Christ.

Jesus alone is the Provider and the perfect example of a God-given character.

. . .

Only Jesus can TRANSFORM a LIAR to an HONEST person, a THIEF to a GIVER, a LAZY person to a HARD WORKER, a WORLDLY HUMAN to a GODLY HUMAN.

The process of developing God-given character traits begins by receiving Jesus as one's personal Savior and Lord.

If you honestly and sincerely try to follow the instructions of this book, your life will be totally transformed.

Do not give up along the way because you do not succeed 100%. Hold out and move onward. Take one small step at a time, and when you experience the joy of succeeding, set yourself higher goals.

WHAT IS CHARACTER DEVELOPMENT?

1. To clarify special character qualities such as HONESTY, GRATEFULNESS, and DILIGENCE and know how they operate in life.

• • •

2. To listen to your CONSCIENCE and COOPERATE with it when it tells you what is right and wrong.

3. To learn how God expects you to RELATE to other people such as family, the church, the workplace, the authorities, and everyone else you meet in life.

4. To develop DISCIPLINE and hold back and master THOUGHTS, WORDS, ACTS, and BEHAVIOR.

5. To give true COMPLIMENTS to others when they demonstrate true character qualities.

6. To learn how to live out the GOLDEN RULE in all areas of life — DO UNTO OTHERS AS YOU WOULD HAVE OTHERS DO UNTO YOU.

• • •

Too many people are afraid to step out of the crowd, afraid to stand out from the rest. It is very important to remember that it is not the MAJORITY and its CONSENT that are the source of true and noble character.

REMEMBER, THE MAJORITY ALWAYS CHANGES ITS OPINIONS TO MATCH THE CURRENT CONDITIONS. It is therefore not always right to follow the majority.

HOW TO MOTIVATE CHARACTER DEVELOPMENT

One of the strongest and best ways to motivate character development is to compliment your fellow human beings.

The praise we give to others helps them achieve their life goals.

Praise is not the same as flattery.

Proverbs 29:5 "Those who flatter their neighbor are spreading nets for their feet."

• • •

Flattery exaggerates the truth with a false motive. Flattery brings PRIDE to the person who is flattered.

Proverbs 25:28 "Like a city whose walls are broken through is a person who lacks self-control."

Your words can lead to your ruin.

Truth and true praise always give birth to humility.
Giving true, genuine, and original praise to others for their good character qualities requires recognizing our own need for this very same quality.

LET ME REMIND YOU THAT JESUS IS THE PERSONALIZATION OF ALL PERFECT CHARACTER.

If we let Jesus work in and through us and we respond correctly to the conditions of our different lives, we develop the CHARACTER OF CHRIST in our lives.

Romans 8:28-29 "**28** And we know that in all things God works for the good of those who love him, who have been called according to his purpose. **29** For those God foreknew he also predestined to be CONFORMED to the IMAGE OF HIS SON, that he might be the firstborn among many brothers and sisters."

2

How Should We Be?

PASS YOUR LIFE TEST.

2ND TIMOTHY 2:15-26 "15 Do your best to present yourself to God as one APPROVED, a worker who does not need to be ashamed and who correctly handles the WORD OF TRUTH…"

1. Stay away from ungodly EMPTY TALK.

2. Become a tool for fine use. HOLY, USEFUL, and APPLICABLE to ALL good work.

3. Shy away from youthful TENDENCIES.

4. Strive for JUSTICE, FAITH, LOVE, and PEACE with those who call on the Lord of a PURE HEART.

5. Stay away from STUPID and HEATED

DISCUSSIONS. A servant of the Lord is not to antagonize anyone.

6. Be FRIENDLY toward everyone. Be a good teacher. Tolerate when someone causes you severe discomfort. Rebuke others with MILDNESS to make them repent.

2 Corinthians 2:14-16 "**14** But thanks be to God, who always leads us as captives in Christ's triumphal procession and uses us to spread the aroma of the knowledge of him everywhere. **15** For we are to God the PLEASING AROMA OF CHRIST among those who are being saved and those who are perishing. **16** To the one we are an aroma that brings death; to the other, an aroma that brings life. And who is equal to such a task?"

1. We must have a sincere, true and original fellowship with Jesus as our Savior and Lord.

2. We must have an understanding that God has called us.

3. We must be people of sound Christian character.

4. Have a teachable spirit.

5. Love Jesus as our Lord and Master.

6. Care about and love people. Have patience with those whom Jesus had and continues to have patience with.

7. Be willing to make sacrifices.

8. Be willing to serve people with true joy.

9. Be willing to work with others also when they do things differently than oneself.

10. Be willing to submit to others and their leadership and authority.

11. Honor and fulfill agreements and promises.

12. Walk in the light and leave all doors open for communication.

13. Share with other people.

14. Be faithful and loyal.

15. Praise the strengths of others.

16. Protect the weak.

17. Support and encourage each other; do not tear each other down.

18. Never sweep things under the rug. Instead, immediately solve the problem in love.

19. Never allow unresolved sin in your life. It gives Satan a foothold through which he will accuse you.

20. You must always look ahead and climb the next mountain. Never dwell on your past.

3

Motivation

CLEAN HEART AND CLEAN HANDS.

YOU HAVE to ask yourself the question: "Why do I do what I do? And who am I doing it for?"

It is important that we always have a CLEAN HEART and CLEAN HANDS. That is, our motives are pure, and so are our actions.

WE MUST HAVE A HEART THAT ATTRACTS GOD'S HEART.

Our title, respect, or so-called great deeds do not give us spiritual authority. Truth and true spirituality are when we are completely controlled by the Holy Spirit.

Spiritual people create people like themselves, not like their words, but as they genuinely are. You transfer "who you are."

God acts on the motivation of our hearts when we do what we do.

WORKMEN.

1st Timothy 3:1-13 clearly states what qualities a leader in the church should have. These are positive goals to have, even if you are not a leader.

So, what should a leader be like?

A leader is…

1. Immaculate.
2. A loyal husband.
3. Sober.
4. Considerate.
5. Worthy.
6. Hospitable.
7. A good teacher.
8. Not a drunk.
9. Not violent.
10. Mild-Tempered.
11. Not belligerent.
12. Not overly fond of money.
13. Manages his house well.

14. Not arrogant.

15. Has a good reputation.

16. Respectable.

17. True to his word.

18. Not beholden to wine.

19. Not greedy.

20. Holds the truth of faith with a clear conscience. (1 Timothy 3:9)

21. Does not gossip.

22. Has faith in all circumstances.

The Bible states, "Those who have served well gain an excellent standing and great assurance in their faith in Christ Jesus." 1 Timothy 3:13

Humility and servitude are two important and necessary things in your life that you must train yourself in every single day.

The result will be GREATNESS that does not have to announce itself.

The HEART and LIFE speak more clearly and

more abundantly than the WORD OF THE TONGUE.

JUDAS AND JESUS.

Matthew 27:3-10 "**3** When Judas, who had betrayed him, saw that Jesus was condemned, he was seized with remorse and returned the thirty pieces of silver to the chief priests and the elders. **4** "I have sinned," he said, "for I have betrayed innocent blood."

"What is that to us?" they replied. "That's your responsibility."

5 So Judas threw the money into the temple and left. Then he went away and hanged himself.

6 The chief priests picked up the coins and said, "It is against the law to put this into the treasury, since it is blood money." **7** So they decided to use the money to buy the potter's field as a burial place for foreigners. **8** That is why it has been called the Field of Blood to this day. **9** Then what was spoken by Jeremiah the prophet was fulfilled: "They took the thirty pieces of silver, the price set on him by the people of Israel, **10** and they used them to buy the potter's field, as the Lord commanded me."

• • •

Judas and Jesus were not just colleagues but close friends and Judas was a trusted friend and co-worker. Judas was Jesus' treasurer and took care of the finances.

ONE WAS LOST, AND THE OTHER BECAME THE KING OF KINGS.

JESUS' MOTIVATION WAS, AND STILL IS, LOVE.

John 15:9-17 "**9** "As the Father has loved me, so have I loved you. Now remain in my love. **10** If you keep my commands, you will remain in my love, just as I have kept my Father's commands and remain in his love. **11** I have told you this so that my joy may be in you and that your joy may be complete. **12** My command is this: Love each other as I have loved you. **13** Greater love has no one than this: to lay down one's life for one's friends. **14** You are my friends if you do what I command. **15** I no longer call you servants, because a servant does not know his master's business. Instead, I have called you friends, for everything that I learned from my Father I have made known to you. **16** You did not choose me, but I chose you and appointed you so that you might go and bear fruit—fruit that will last

—and so that whatever you ask in my name the Father will give you. **17** This is my command: Love each other."

JUDAS' MOTIVATION WAS HIS EGO.

Judas thought only of himself. It was a personal desire for financial enrichment that drove him. "What will you give me?"

Matthew 26:14-16 "**14** Then one of the Twelve—the one called Judas Iscariot—went to the chief priests **15** and asked, "What are you willing to give me if I deliver him over to you?" So, they counted out for him thirty pieces of silver. **16** From then on Judas watched for an opportunity to hand him over."

The archangel, Satan, had the same motivation.

HOW CAN YOU RECOGNIZE LOVE VERSUS DESIRE?

LOVE: Always gives to others and always wants to give, regardless of the price or cost.

DESIRE: Always wants personal gain, even at the expense of others.

Faith and love always work together. Faith always attracts the positive.

Desire and fear go hand in hand and always create disbelief. Fear always attracts the negative.

THE SPIRIT OF JUDAH.

2 Kings 5:20-27 "**20** Gehazi, the servant of Elisha the man of God, said to himself, "My master was too easy on Naaman, this Aramean, by not accepting from him what he brought. As surely as the Lord lives, I will run after him and get something from him."

21 So Gehazi hurried after Naaman. When Naaman saw him running toward him, he got down from the chariot to meet him. "Is everything all right?" he asked.

22 "Everything is all right," Gehazi answered. "My master sent me to say, 'Two young men from the company of the prophets have just come to me from the hill country of Ephraim. Please give them a talent of silver and two sets of clothing.'"

Eagle or Chicken

23 "By all means, take two talents," said Naaman. He urged Gehazi to accept them, and then tied up the two talents of silver in two bags, with two sets of clothing. He gave them to two of his servants, and they carried them ahead of Gehazi. **24** When Gehazi came to the hill, he took the things from the servants and put them away in the house. He sent the men away and they left.

25 When he went in and stood before his master, Elisha asked him, "Where have you been, Gehazi?"

"Your servant didn't go anywhere," Gehazi answered.

26 But Elisha said to him, "Was not my spirit with you when the man got down from his chariot to meet you? Is this the time to take money or to accept clothes—or olive groves and vineyards, or flocks and herds, or male and female slaves? **27** Naaman's leprosy will cling to you and to your descendants forever." Then Gehazi went from Elisha's presence and his skin was leprous—it had become as white as snow."

GEHAZI WAS GREEDY AND EAGER TO ACCEPT THE OFFER. GREED ALWAYS CREATES LIES. LIES ARE PUNISHED.

SIMON "THE GREAT" WIZARD.

Acts 8:9-24 "**9** Now for some time a man named Simon had practiced sorcery in the city and amazed all the people of Samaria. He boasted that he was someone great, **10** and all the people, both high and low, gave him their attention and exclaimed, "This man is rightly called the Great Power of God." **11** They followed him because he had amazed them for a long time with his sorcery. **12** But when they believed Philip as he proclaimed the good news of the kingdom of God and the name of Jesus Christ, they were baptized, both men and women. **13** Simon himself believed and was baptized. And he followed Philip everywhere, astonished by the great signs and miracles he saw.

14 When the apostles in Jerusalem heard that Samaria had accepted the Word of God, they sent Peter and John to Samaria. **15** When they arrived, they prayed for the new believers there that they might receive the Holy Spirit, **16** because the Holy Spirit had not yet come on any of them; they had simply been baptized in the name of the Lord Jesus. **17** Then Peter and John placed their hands on them, and they received the Holy Spirit.

18 When Simon saw that the Spirit was given at

the laying on of the apostles' hands, he offered them money **19** and said, "Give me also this ability so that everyone on whom I lay my hands may receive the Holy Spirit."

20 Peter answered: "May your money perish with you, because you thought you could buy the gift of God with money! **21** You have no part or share in this ministry, because your heart is not right before God. **22** Repent of this wickedness and pray to the Lord in the hope that he may forgive you for having such a thought in your heart. **23** For I see that you are full of bitterness and captive to sin."

24 Then Simon answered, "Pray to the Lord for me so that nothing you have said may happen to me."

SIMON TROLDMAND pretended to be someone bigger than he was. HE WAS FULL OF PRIDE AND THOUGHT HE COULD BUY GOD'S GIFT WITH MONEY.

Signs and wonders are not signs of true spirituality, and true spirituality cannot be bought for money.

With his money, Simon the Wizard wanted to buy himself back into the center of people's lives.

YES, AMONG YOURSELVES.

Acts 20:28-31 "**28** Keep watch over yourselves and all the flock of which the Holy Spirit has made you overseers. Be shepherds of the church of God, which he bought with his own blood. **29** I know that after I leave, savage wolves will come in among you and will not spare the flock. **30** Even from your own number men will arise and distort the truth in order to draw away disciples after them. **31** So be on your guard! Remember that for three years I never stopped warning each of you night and day with tears."

SAVAGE WOLVES ARE PEOPLE WHO SEEK INFLUENCE, CONTROL, AND POWER OVER OTHER PEOPLE'S LIVES. THEY DESIRE A FEELING OF POWER.

But we must both love and serve God and people from a pure heart and motive.

4

We Must Learn To Lead Ourselves Before We Can Lead Others

THE HEAD, NOT THE TAIL.

THE BIBLE TEACHES us in Deuteronomy 28:13 that we should be the "head" and not the "tail."

In Genesis 1:28, we see that God blessed man and said that we should commit ourselves to ruling the Earth.

This applies to all of us, and it is important we do it from a pure heart, with true and honest motives.

1. We must have the ability to "influence" others positively.

2. It has nothing to do with who you are and what you do, but it is a matter of becoming "who you are."

3. As children of God, we are created to be led by the Spirit of God.

4. It is not your title that makes you a leader.

5. A true leader is always willing to suffer for the cause. Jesus did.

6. A leader will always bring the best out in other people and inspire them to give all they can.

7. Leadership must be learned; it is a growth process.

8. We must be motivated by love for God and people and not by ambitions to become great.

9. Always remember that only God can give true spiritual authority.

10. Be faithful in small things, and you will come to "rule" over a lot.

11. Always be a giver.

12. Follow through on every word you speak.

13. Learn how best to serve other people.

14. You must pray and study the Word of God to gain wisdom.

15. You must learn to be kind, but with determination.

16. You must have generosity and trust.

17. You must be above all reproach and criticism.

18. You must lead your family properly and well.

19. You must always be willing to learn more.

20. You must never be motivated by money.

21. Truth and true character are created in the hidden, crafted in your private life, and observed in public life.

22. You must be willing to stand alone.

23. Pay the price in its entirety, 100%.

24. You must work more than all the others.

25. Be aware that you are "only" part of a long chain. There is a past, present, and future.

26. A true leader sees the world when others only see the village.

The Bible says in Ephesians 6:7 to "serve WHOLEHEARTEDLY, as if you were serving the Lord, not people."

In everything we do, even if we do it for other people, we must do it with excellence and do it in such a way that God Himself will be pleased with us. We must therefore always cling to the Lord

WHOLEHEARTEDLY and be filled with the HOLY SPIRIT AND FAITH. Acts 11:23-24.

We must always seek and earnestly strive (desire wholeheartedly) to become a man after GOD'S HEART. Such a man will come to do ALL that GOD WANTS. Acts 13:22.

BECOME A PERSON WHO IS FAITHFUL THROUGH TRIALS AND TEMPTATIONS.

James 1:2-8 "**2** Consider it pure joy, my brothers and sisters, whenever you face trials of many kinds, **3** because you know that the testing of your faith produces perseverance. **4** Let perseverance finish its work so that you may be mature and complete, not lacking anything. **5** If any of you lacks wisdom, you should ask God, who gives generously to all without finding fault, and it will be given to you. **6** But when you ask, you must believe and not doubt, because the one who doubts is like a wave of the sea, blown and tossed by the wind. **7** That person should not expect to receive anything from the Lord. **8** Such a person is double-minded and unstable in all they do."

. . .

1. Wake up!!

Decide every morning when you wake up that this day will be the best in your life.

Psalms 118:24 "The Lord has done it this very day; let us rejoice today and be glad."

2. Get dressed!!

The best attire you can put on is a big smile. A smile costs nothing, but it adorns your outward appearance.

1 Samuel 16:7 "But the Lord said to Samuel, "Do not consider his appearance or his height, for I have rejected him. The Lord does not look at the things people look at. People look at the outward appearance, but the Lord looks at the heart."

3. Be quiet!!

Speak only good words and learn to listen to others. God gave us two ears and a mouth, so he likely meant we should listen twice as much as we talk.

Proverbs 13:3 "Those who guard their lips

preserve their lives, but those who speak rashly will come to ruin."

4. Stand up!!

Dare to stand up for what you believe in. If you do not stand up for something, you will fall.

Galatians 6:9-10 "**9** Let us not become weary in doing good, for at the proper time we will reap a harvest if we do not give up. **10** Therefore, as we have opportunity, let us do good to all people, especially to those who belong to the family of believers."

5. Look up!!

Always look up to God and your Savior, Jesus Christ.

Philippians 4:13 "I can do all this through him who gives me strength."

6. Reach upwards!!

Reach out and up for something higher and bigger.

Proverbs 3:5-6 "**5** Trust in the Lord with all your

heart and lean not on your own understanding; **6** in all your ways submit to him, and he will make your paths straight."

7. Lift up!!

Raise your prayers to the Lord, our God.

Philippians 4:6 "Do not be anxious about anything, but in every situation, by prayer and petition, with thanksgiving, present your requests to God."

Do you need anything? Then you must learn to pray in faith and trust that God not only hears your prayer but will also answer your prayer. You must not be ambivalent and unsteady in your life. Make the path of faith your lifestyle.

LEARN TO BE HAPPY IN ALL CIRCUMSTANCES.

5

Character Traits And Leadership

1. You can only lead others as far as you have come yourself.
2. You must endure criticism and unkind talk.
3. You must be courageous and brave.
4. You must first learn to stand alone so that others will stand by you.
5. You must be willing to "pay" the price in "silence" for strenuous effort, struggle, resistance, misunderstanding, etc. The most important thing is personal holiness and spiritual anointing in your life.
6. You must develop a vision and strong character traits.

7. Strong character traits are not "gifts" but results.
8. Do not see yourself as you are NOW, but as God your Creator sees you.
9. A strong character organizes and coordinates resources, energy, and relationships to achieve results.
10. A strong character creates compassion and passion for accomplishing and completing life's tasks.
11. Having a strong character removes the focus from your sense of self.
12. Strong character traits do more than maintain; they develop and produce.
13. A strong character has the ability not only to rectify one's own "failures" but also those of others.
14. True character calls for respect, not just from friends but also from enemies.
15. True character always seeks to reconcile opposition without accusation and without compromise.
16. True character affects the next generation.
17. True character will protect your heart

and life by never compromising to avoid losing your credibility and respect.

WORLDLY CHARACTER	SPIRITUAL CHARACTER
Self-absorbed	Trust in and preoccupation with God
Know only mankind	Know both mankind and God.
Make their own decisions	Seek God's will
Ambitious	Self-Sacrificing
Organizes own methods	Knows God's methods
Wants to "command" others	Is happy to serve other people
Motivated by personal interests	Motivated by love
Independent	Independent in God

THE PRICE FOR TRUTHFUL CHARACTER TRAITS.

1. Personal sacrifice.
2. Rejection and being cast out.
3. Criticism, vicious talk, and attacks.
4. Being complicated and confused.
5. Mental and physical fatigue and exhaustion.
6. Loneliness.
7. Being made a "victim" of others.

DANGERS OF DEVELOPING TRUTHFUL CHARACTER TRAITS.

1. Popularity.
2. Pride.
3. Self-centeredness and indispensability.

WITH TRUE SPIRITUAL character in your life, you have the COURAGE to react when all others hesitate.

With true spiritual character in your life, you will have the ABILITY to identify the problem before it turns into a crisis.

With true spiritual character in your life, you will be GREAT enough to acknowledge your mistakes, SMART enough to profit from them, and STRONG enough to correct them.

ALWAYS REMEMBER THAT WHAT REALLY COUNTS IN LIFE ARE NOT TITLES,

BUT CHARACTER.

IT IS NOT THE PERSON BUT THE CHARACTER TRAITS.

GREAT PEOPLE ARE VERY ORDINARY PEOPLE WHO NEVER GIVE UP.

6

The Right Attitude Is Mandatory

The right attitude may seem like a small thing, BUT IT MAKES A BIG DIFFERENCE.

THE RIGHT ATTITUDE is like a small rock being thrown into the ocean and creating ripples that just get bigger and bigger as they spread.

Philippians 2:4-5 "...not looking to your own interests but each of you to the interests of the others. **5** In your relationships with one another, have the same mindset as Christ Jesus."

With almost any kind of "item" you buy today, a manual is included to teach us how to operate and use the new "item" in the best, most efficient way for the user's enjoyment.

God has given us a manual for life, the BIBLE, which shows us what attitude (mentality) we should have in our lives.

Jesus is our greatest and best example to follow. His high standard is not meant to frustrate us but rather reveal areas in our lives that we should change or improve.

Jesus was not selfish. Jesus had the right image of himself and was therefore secure. Jesus surrendered completely to the calling of His life.

The result of a fresh attitude and mentality is to do the will of God in one's life.

The right attitude always leads to the right actions and lifestyle.

Romans 12:1-2 "1 Therefore, I urge you, brothers and sisters, in view of God's mercy, to offer your bodies as a living sacrifice, holy and pleasing to God—this is your true and proper worship. 2 Do not conform to the pattern of this world but be transformed by the renewing of your mind. Then you will be able to test and approve what God's will is—his good, pleasing and perfect will."

KEEP THE RIGHT ATTITUDE WHEN THINGS BECOME DIFFICULT.

Our attitude is most important when we are going through crises and having difficulties. All too often, we "check out" to compensate for our problems.

The worst thing you can do in difficult situations is panic because you will make the wrong decisions.

When you go "down" and collapse, it is most often due to a wrong reaction, not because your life is turbulent.

ALL TOO OFTEN, SMALL THINGS ARE BLOWN OUT OF PROPORTION.

What really matters is what happens "inside us" and not "with us." When the external conditions lead to wrong internal reactions, we have a real problem.

In 2 Timothy 3:11, Paul says, "...persecutions, sufferings—what kinds of things happened to me in Antioch, Iconium and Lystra, the persecutions I endured. Yet the Lord rescued me from all of them."

In verse 12, he goes on to say, "In fact, everyone who wants to live a godly life in Christ Jesus will be persecuted."

PAUL ALLOWED THE DIFFICULT AND POWERFUL STORMS OF LIFE TO MAKE HIMSELF STRONGER.

James actually tells us that life's problems and challenges are good for us.

James 1:2-4 "**2** Consider it pure joy, my brothers and sisters, whenever you face trials of many kinds, **3** because you know that the testing of your faith produces perseverance. **4** Let perseverance finish its work so that you may be mature and complete, not lacking anything."

THE STORM OF LIFE DOES NOT LAST FOREVER.

When life is difficult, we often forget the "truth" and become preoccupied with the problems. The radiance of our lives is colored by the present.

A drowning person is not preoccupied with the tasks of tomorrow.

When everything looks hopeless, and you say, "now, I've had enough," instead, train yourself to believe and say, "this too shall pass."

IT IS NOT THE SIZE OF THE PROBLEM BUT THE DURATION OF THE PROBLEM THAT WEARS US OUT.

Galatians 6:9 "Let us not become weary in doing good, for at the proper time we will reap a harvest if we do not give up."

It is possible to lose your harvest by not enduring.

For a marathon runner, the first part of the race is the hardest; it really hurts. But after the pain comes a renewed strength to continue, and it gets easier and easier the closer you get to the finish line.

Hebrews 12:1-3 "**1** Therefore, since we are surrounded by such a great cloud of witnesses, let us throw off everything that hinders and the sin that so easily entangles. And let us run with perseverance the race marked out for us, **2** fixing our eyes on Jesus, the pioneer and perfecter of faith. For the joy set before him he endured the cross, scorning its shame, and sat down at the right hand of the throne of God. **3** Consider him who endured such opposition from sinners, so that you will not grow weary and lose heart."

MAKE THE BIG AND CRITICAL DECISIONS BEFORE THE STORM COMES.

Many storms can be avoided by "thinking" and "planning" well in advance. Do not be indifferent and just let things "go their way."

All too often, we blame the Devil for our problems, but often it is ourselves who are the "devil." It also does not help much to resist the Devil if it is yourself who is an obstacle to solving the problems.

NOT ALL PROBLEMS CAN BE PREVENTED.

WHAT DO WE DO IN STORMY WEATHER?

STORM INDICATOR:

1. You have no experience. If you know someone who has experience, ask them for help.

2. You have no knowledge. Have you prepared yourself by studying and being willing to learn?

3. You are short of time. Do you prioritize and use the time right?

4. You don't know the facts. Have you seriously investigated the situation?

5. You are not praying enough. Is it your idea or

God's idea? Is God blessing you by giving you His support and confirmation?

WHEN IT'S STORMING, YOU HAVE TO MAKE DECISIONS, BUT IT IS IMPORTANT TO DO SO AT THE RIGHT TIME.

1. The wrong decision at the wrong time leads to disaster.
2. The wrong decision at the right time leads to mistakes.
3. The right decision at the wrong time is unacceptable.
4. THE RIGHT DECISION AT THE RIGHT TIME ALWAYS LEADS TO SUCCESS.

Never let circumstances control your way of thinking. Your way of thinking determines your decisions. Make your decisions when life is calm.

ALWAYS BE IN CONTACT WITH THE CONTROL TOWER.

Every pilot in an aircraft always appreciates the contact with the control tower on the ground, even though he ultimately controls the aircraft and makes the decisions.

All too often, we will do things ourselves without seeking any kind of help. But then we also have ourselves to thank when things turn out badly.

In John 15, Jesus says the following:

4 Remain in me, as I also remain in you. No branch can bear fruit by itself; it must remain in the vine. Neither can you bear fruit unless you remain in me.

5 "I am the vine; you are the branches. If you remain in me and I in you, you will bear much fruit; apart from me you can do nothing. **6** If you do not remain in me, you are like a branch that is thrown away and withers; such branches are picked up, thrown into the fire and burned. **7** If you remain in me and my words remain in you, ask whatever you wish, and it will be done for you.

FEAR OF FAILURE.

Too many people will deny that they fear not succeeding in this life. They hide their fears. They deny their fears. They ignore their fears. They hate their fears, and they "fear" their fears.

None of this will help. If you are full of fear and you want to succeed in your life, you must dare to come face to face with your fears.

HE WHO NEVER MAKES MISTAKES IN LIFE WILL ALSO NEVER ACHIEVE ANYTHING IN LIFE.

The vast majority of "great" people who have accomplished something in their lives and for their fellow human beings made many mistakes.

Your first attempt rarely succeeds.

Henry Ford forgot to add the reverse gear in the first car.

WE MUST ACCEPT MISTAKES IN LIFE AS A VERY IMPORTANT PROCESS IN REACHING OUR LIFE'S GOALS.

No one can succeed without pain, not even you. If you have succeeded without pain, then others have suffered on your behalf.

It is important that you remember that God wants you to succeed, and He suffered for you so that you can reach your life goal.

Psalm 1:1-3

1 Blessed is the one who does not walk in step with the wicked or stand in the way that sinners take or sit in the company of mockers, **2** but whose delight is in the law of the Lord, and who meditates on his law day and night.

3 That person is like a tree planted by streams of water, which yields its fruit in season and whose leaf does not wither—WHATEVER THEY DO PROSPERS.

Jesus taught and demonstrated this truth.

• • •

John 12:24-25

24 Very truly I tell you, unless a kernel of wheat falls to the ground and dies, it remains only a single seed. But if it dies, it produces many seeds. **25** Anyone who loves their life will lose it, while anyone who hates their life in this world will keep it for eternal life."

John 15:13 "Greater love has no one than this: to lay down one's life for one's friends."

Paul says in Galatians 2:20, "I have been crucified with Christ and I no longer live, but Christ lives in me. The life I now live in the body, I live by faith in the Son of God, who loved me and gave himself for me."

NO ONE CAN SUCCEED IN LIFE WITHOUT TAKING RISKS. THOSE WHO DO NOT WANT TO RISK ANYTHING IN LIFE "DO NOTHING, HAVE NOTHING, AND ARE NOTHING."

. . .

Accepting "failure" as the final result will also lead to final and conclusive failure.

WINNERS ARE PEOPLE WHO NEVER GIVE UP.

7

The 7 Deadly Sins

OUR ATTITUDE IS NOT AUTOMATICALLY **good** because we are Christians.

There are seven different kinds of sins that will kill you if allowed to do so. They are as follows:

1. Pride.
2. Greed.
3. Lust.
4. Envy.
5. Wrath.
6. Gluttony, excess.
7. Laziness.

These sins are the result of a bad attitude, inner spirit, and motivation.

. . .

In Luke 15:11-32, we find the parable of the prodigal son where it says the following:

"**11** Jesus continued: "There was a man who had two sons. **12** The younger one said to his father, 'Father, give me my share of the estate.' So, he divided his property between them.

13 "Not long after that, the younger son got together all he had, set off for a distant country and there squandered his wealth in wild living. **14** After he had spent everything, there was a severe famine in that whole country, and he began to be in need. **15** So he went and hired himself out to a citizen of that country, who sent him to his fields to feed pigs. **16** He longed to fill his stomach with the pods that the pigs were eating, but no one gave him anything.

17 "When he came to his senses, he said, 'How many of my father's hired servants have food to spare, and here I am starving to death! **18** I will set out and go back to my father and say to him: Father, I have sinned against heaven and against you. **19** I am no longer worthy to be called your son; make me like one of your hired servants.' **20** So he got up and went to his father.

"But while he was still a long way off, his father saw him and was filled with compassion for him; he ran to his son, threw his arms around him and kissed him.

21 "The son said to him, 'Father, I have sinned against heaven and against you. I am no longer worthy to be called your son.'

22 "But the father said to his servants, 'Quick! Bring the best robe and put it on him. Put a ring on his finger and sandals on his feet. **23** Bring the fattened calf and kill it. Let's have a feast and celebrate. **24** For this son of mine was dead and is alive again; he was lost and is found.' So, they began to celebrate.

25 "Meanwhile, the older son was in the field. When he came near the house, he heard music and dancing. **26** So he called one of the servants and asked him what was going on. **27** 'Your brother has come,' he replied, 'and your father has killed the fattened calf because he has him back safe and sound.'

28 "The older brother became angry and refused to go in. So, his father went out and pleaded with him. **29** But he answered his father, 'Look! All these years I've been slaving for you and never disobeyed your orders. Yet you never gave me even a young goat so I could celebrate with my friends. **30** But when this son of yours who has squandered your property with prostitutes comes home, you kill the fattened calf for him!'

31 "'My son,' the father said, 'you are always with me, and everything I have is yours. **32** But we had to celebrate and be glad, because this brother of yours was dead and is alive again; he was lost and is found.'"

When the youngest and prodigal son "came home," the eldest son revealed a bad attitude.

1. He was conceited.

2. He displayed his self-pity and felt bad for himself.

In this story, we find not only one prodigal son but two.

A. The youngest: GUILTY IN THE SIN OF THE FLESH.

B. The Eldest: GUILTY IN SPIRITUAL (ATTITUDE) SIN.

When the parable ends, it is the eldest son who is outside the father's house.

FIVE IMPORTANT THINGS IN A PROPER CHRISTIAN ATTITUDE AND BEHAVIOR.

Philippians 2:3-8 "**3** Do nothing out of selfish ambition or vain conceit. Rather, in humility value others above yourselves, **4** not looking to your own interests but each of you to the interests of the others. **5** In your relationships with one another, have the same mindset as Christ Jesus: **6** Who, being in very nature God, did not consider equality with God something to be used to his own advantage; **7** rather, he made himself nothing by taking the very nature of a servant, being made in human likeness. **8** And being found in appearance as a man, he humbled himself by becoming obedient to death — even death on a cross!"

1. Have the right motivations in everything we do.

2. With humility, always put others higher than yourself.

3. Do not think of yourself and yours, but what is best for others.

4. Jesus knew that He embodied the characteristics of God, that he is the Son of God, and yet is still willing to serve others, including you.

5. Always seek and adopt the "Christ-like attitude," which is never power-hungry but calls upon and demonstrates obedience and fulfills God's purpose and goals.

THE ATTITUDE OF THE ELDEST BROTHER HAS 3 NEGATIVE RESULTS.

1. He had all the rights of the father in the house, and his outward conduct was correct, but his attitude was wrong, and his fellowship with the father was damaged. Luke 15:28.
2. It is possible to serve the father faithfully and yet not have fellowship with him. He did not understand why the father could rejoice in the return of his youngest son.
3. It is possible to be the heir to all the father's property and yet lose the joy and the freedom.

The servants were happier and freer than the older brother. They ate, laughed, and danced while he stood outside, was angry, and demanded his right.

The wrong attitude kept him away from his father's heart's desire, the love of his younger brother, and the joy of the servants.

HAVING THE WRONG ATTITUDE WILL BLOCK AND PREVENT YOU FROM RECEIVING GOD'S BLESSING AND CAUSE

YOU TO LIVE FAR BELOW GOD'S STAN-
DARD FOR YOUR LIFE.

IF YOU BEGIN TO LOOK LIKE THE OLDEST SON, REMEMBER TWO VERY IMPORTANT THINGS.

1. Your privilege: "'My son,' the father said, 'you are always with me." Luke 15:31
2. Your inheritance: "…and everything I have is yours." Luke 15:31

Just take a moment and think about how privileged you really are and how many promises of God's blessing you have.

Pray the same prayer as Jabez:

1 Chronicles 4:10 "Jabez cried out to the God of Israel, "Oh, that you would bless me and enlarge my territory! Let your hand be with me and keep me from harm so that I will be free from pain." And God granted his request.

GOD HEARD HIS PRAYER, AND GOD GAVE HIM WHAT HE ASKED FOR.

8

12 Foundations Of Quality Character

To develop and train mature and successful men and women to achieve the highest form of efficiency and productivity in work and lifestyle, it is important and necessary to integrate the following character qualities into all aspects of daily life.

1. Attention versus distraction.

Recognize a person's value by paying attention.

2. Obedience versus self-centeredness.

Receive instruction, correction, reward, and protection under the leadership of parents, civilian authorities, employers, and church leaders.

3. Gratitude versus pride.

Communicate to others the precise and noble way in which they have enriched you and find a way to honor them.

4. Truth versus deception.

Receive future trust by carefully reporting past facts.

5. Order versus confusion.

Organize everything in your life to serve the purpose for which it was created.

6. Diligence versus laziness.

Demonstrate your dedication to the visions and goals of your authorities (leaders) by using all your energy to complete your work tasks.

7. Punctuality versus disorder.

Know and value time and develop a plan to complete your responsibilities.

8. Ingenuity versus being wasteful.

Apply wisdom to use what others usually overlook and discard.

9. Caring versus indifference.

Get to know what will ruin your work effectiveness and avoid neglectful words.

10. Patience versus frustration.

Pay attention and see values in circumstances that you cannot change. Invest the necessary time and energy in changing the conditions you can.

11. Honesty versus hypocrisy.

Strive for excellence with an open mind when it comes to your personal needs and weaknesses.

12. Generosity versus selfishness.

Be aware that everything you have and own has been given to you; therefore, use it to enrich and bless as many people as possible.

9

44 Quality Traits Everyone Should Develop

1. Attention versus inattention.
2. Satisfaction versus dissatisfaction.
3. Diligence versus laziness.
4. Flexibility versus negative resistance.
5. Being present versus indifferent.
6. Creativity versus unproductivity.
7. Level-headed versus quick to judgment.
8. Forgiveness versus rejection.
9. Accessible versus self-centered.
10. Decisive versus ambiguous.
11. Restrained versus brash.
12. Bold versus timid.
13. Polite versus coarse.
14. Perseverance versus quitting.
15. Mild versus hard.

16. Well thought out versus hasty.
17. Determination versus indecision.
18. Hospitality versus seclusion.
19. Humility versus pride.
20. Obedience versus stubbornness.
21. Responsible versus untrustworthy.
22. Thoroughness versus incompetence.
23. Initiative versus indifference.
24. Organized versus disorganized.
25. Respectful versus disrespectful.
26. Frugality versus wastefulness.
27. Joyful versus self-pity.
28. Patience versus impatience.
29. Certainty versus indecision.
30. Tolerance versus intolerance.
31. Justice versus injustice.
32. Genuinely paying attention versus self-preoccupation.
33. Self-control versus vagueness.
34. Honesty versus deception.
35. Love versus selfishness.
36. Punctuality versus disorder.
37. Sensitive versus insensitive.
38. Purity versus impurity.
39. Loyalty versus disloyalty.
40. Ingenuity versus sloppiness.

41. Honesty versus hypocrisy.
42. Wisdom versus human desire.
43. Meekness versus short-tempered.
44. Generosity versus stinginess.
45. Having faith versus making assumptions.

JESUS CHRIST IS the very personification of all perfect character traits. When Jesus works in you as you demonstrate the right response to your circumstances, you develop HIS characteristics in your life.

The Bible says in Romans 8:28-29, "And we know that in all things God works for the good of those who love him ... to be conformed to the image of his Son ..."

10

60 Traits That Characterize Jesus

HE IS...

1. Grateful	21. Effective	41. Peaceful
2. Pays Attention	22. Just	42. Persevering
3. Available	23. Fair	43. Convincing
4. Surrendered	24. Faithful	44. Clever
5. Supportive	25. Fearless	45. Punctual
6. Caring	26. Forgiving	46. Determined
7. Trusting	27. Constructive	47. Inventive
8. Thoughtful	28. Friendly	48. Respectful
9. Consistent	29. Generous	49. Responsible
10. Satisfied	30. Mild	50. Provides safety
11. Cooperative	31. Honest	51. Self-controlled
12. Brave	32. Humble	52. Sincere
13. Creative	33. Joyful	53. Obedient
14. Decisive	34. Good	54. Tactful
15. Honorable	35. Loyal	55. Moderate
16. Credible	36. Meek	56. Complete
17. Virtuous	37. Merciful	57. Thrifty
18. Thorough	38. Compassionate	58. Tolerant
19. Insightful	39. Optimistic	59. True
20. Discreet	40. Patient	60. Wise

JESUS IS THE GREATEST EXAMPLE OF HUMANITY, AND HIS EXAMPLE SHOULD BE FOLLOWED.

11

Authenticity Is Worth As Much As Gold

1. Your love for God and people must be genuine.

1 Corinthians 13, called "the love letter," must be the guideline for you in all aspects of life.

"**1** If I speak in the tongues of men or of angels, but do not have love, I am only a resounding gong or a clanging cymbal. **2** If I have the gift of prophecy and can fathom all mysteries and all knowledge, and if I have a faith that can move mountains, but do not have love, I am nothing. **3** If I give all I possess to the poor and give over my body to hardship that I may boast, but do not have love, I gain nothing.

4 Love is patient, love is kind. It does not envy, it does not boast, it is not proud. **5** It does not dishonor others, it is not self-seeking, it is not easily angered, it keeps no record of wrongs. **6** Love does not delight in evil but rejoices with the truth. **7** It always protects, always trusts, always hopes, always perseveres.

8 Love never fails. But where there are prophecies, they will cease; where there are tongues, they will be stilled; where there is knowledge, it will pass away. **9** For we know in part, and we prophesy in part, **10** but when completeness comes, what is in part disappears. **11** When I was a child, I talked like a child, I thought like a child, I reasoned like a child. When I became a man, I put the ways of childhood behind me. **12** For now we see only a reflection as in a mirror; then we shall see face to face. Now I know in part; then I shall know fully, even as I am fully known.

13 AND NOW THESE THREE REMAIN: FAITH, HOPE AND LOVE. BUT THE GREATEST OF THESE IS LOVE."

Be careful with your words and the way you express yourself. Let your speech always express the love that lives in you.

. . .

2. Your worship of God must always be genuine.

John 4:22-24 **"22** You Samaritans worship what you do not know; we worship what we do know, for salvation is from the Jews. **23** Yet a time is coming and has now come when the true worshipers will worship the Father in the Spirit and in truth, for they are the kind of worshipers the Father seeks. **24** God is Spirit, and his worshipers must worship in the Spirit and in truth."

It must be the genuine worship and praise from your heart, not the songbook, that you extend to the Father. Worship must be truly spontaneous, not just traditions.

3. Your prayer life must be genuine.

You must learn to renew your relationship with God through a genuine prayer life. You are responsible for keeping the fire burning. Do not in any way expect that others should do this for you. You must learn to maintain your prayer life as an indispensable part of your lifestyle.

. . .

4. Your speech should always express the truth and be honest and genuine.

James 3 tells us how dangerous our words can be. But if one does not fail in speech, he is

capable of controlling the rest of his body.

JAMES 3:1-12

"**1** Not many of you should become teachers, my fellow believers, because you know that we who teach will be judged more strictly. **2** We all stumble in many ways. Anyone who is never at fault in what they say is perfect, able to keep their whole body in check.

3 When we put bits into the mouths of horses to make them obey us, we can turn the whole animal. **4** Or take ships as an example. Although they are so large and are driven by strong winds, they are steered by a very small rudder wherever the pilot wants to go. **5** Likewise, the tongue is a small part of the body, but it makes great boasts. Consider what a great forest is set on fire by a small spark. **6** The tongue also is a fire, a world of evil among the parts of the body. It corrupts the whole body, sets the whole course of one's life on fire, and is itself set on fire by hell.

7 All kinds of animals, birds, reptiles and sea creatures are being tamed and have been tamed by mankind, **8** but no human being can tame the tongue. It is a restless evil, full of deadly poison.

9 With the tongue we praise our Lord and Father, and with it we curse human beings, who have been made in God's likeness. **10** Out of the same mouth come praise and cursing. My brothers and sisters, this should not be. **11** Can both fresh water and saltwater flow from the same spring? **12** My brothers and sisters, can a fig tree bear olive, or a grapevine bear figs? Neither can a salt spring produce fresh water."

YOU MUST STRIVE TO BE ABLE TO SPEAK WITHOUT ERROR.

5. Your behavior must always be genuine.

The way I act with my family at home, at work, among friends, and in the church must radiate authenticity.

Your body language must be genuine when you meet people; you must be authentic and always reflect Jesus Christ.

. . .

6. Your joy must reflect true authenticity.

The Bible teaches us to always rejoice in the Lord in all circumstances. You must demonstrate

the radiance of joy even if things go against you and your patience is tested.

Proverbs 17:22 "A CHEERFUL HEART IS GOOD MEDICINE, BUT A CRUSHED SPIRIT DRIES UP THE BONES."

7. Your decisions must always be genuine.

When you decide something, you must mean it. When God speaks to you through his servants, via the Word of God, or otherwise, it must be a WILLFUL DECISION, NOT A SUPERFICIAL THOUGHT.

IF YOU ARE NOT GENUINE IN YOUR DECISIONS, GOD CANNOT COME AND HELP YOU.

YOUR AUTHENTICITY WILL OPEN YOUR LIFE FOR GOD'S BLESSINGS.

Let your true, genuine, and spiritual character and attitude lead you into a lively and enriching fellowship with your Savior and Lord Jesus Christ.

Remember that a neglected Savior will be a stern judge on the Day of Judgment when you have to "account" for your life.

MOST CHRISTIANS GIVE THEIR BODIES THREE MEALS OF FOOD PER DAY, THEIR SPIRIT A COLD LUNCH ONCE A WEEK, AND THEN WONDER WHY GOD DOESN'T DO MORE FOR THEM.

A TRUE CHRISTIAN WILL TAKE JUST AS MUCH TAKE CARE OF HIS SPIRIT AS HIS BODY, AS HE KNOWS THAT THE BODY WILL PERISH, BUT THE SPIRIT LIVES ETERNALLY.

It is entirely possible to achieve the same level of character as the great figures in the Bible. You just must be genuine and dedicate yourself as they did. If you do, you will enjoy the same trust in and from the Almighty God as they did.

The authenticity and character standard you must reach is Christ himself.

It is very easy to be ordinary. But one who is genuine and allows himself to be filled with the word and Spirit of God will always be extraordinary.

Never settle for anything but the best, which is what God wants for you. Do not fear criticism because those who want to avoid criticism just must do three things:

1. Do nothing.
2. Be nothing.
3. Say nothing.

Always remember that God doesn't have space for those who look back, think back, and act back.

Also, do not be influenced by what you see and hear BUT BY WHAT YOU BELIEVE.

IT IS BETTER TO DIE TRUSTING IN GOD THAN LIVE IN UNBELIEF.

Be imbued with the Word and Spirit of God so that every fiber of your life has received the full armoring from the Spirit.

If you are "abused" or pushed against the wall, the true character of God in you will show the nature of Christ.

12

10 Rules That Lead To Miraculous Character Development

2 KINGS 4:1-7 "1 The wife of a man from the company of the prophets cried out to Elisha, "Your servant my husband is dead, and you know that he revered the Lord. But now his creditor is coming to take my two boys as his slaves." 2 Elisha replied to her, "How can I help you? Tell me, what do you have in your house?" "Your servant has nothing there at all," she said, "except a small jar of olive oil." 3 Elisha said, "Go around and ask all your neighbors for empty jars. Don't ask for just a few. 4 Then go inside and shut the door behind you and your sons. Pour oil into all the jars, and as each is filled, put it to one side." 5 She left him and shut the door behind her and her sons. They brought the jars to

her, and she kept pouring. **6** When all the jars were full, she said to her son, "Bring me another one." But he replied, "There is not a jar left." Then the oil stopped flowing. **7** She went and told the man of God, and he said, "Go, sell the oil and pay your debts. You and your sons can live on what is left."

1. Know where to turn for help when you do not know what to do.

2. Never seek a "worldly Messiah."

3. Find out what you have in your house.

4. Do not be blinded by negativism, but always be positive.

5. Faith is not faith until you do something. Action is needed.

6. Never let your limitations hinder God's possibilities. Remember, God makes the impossible possible.

7. Always close the door on doubt.

8. Pour until there is no more oil.

9. Work hard and purposefully, despite the miracles.

10. REMEMBER, THERE WILL ALWAYS BE ENOUGH!

IF YOU SET THESE RULES FOR YOUR LIFE, YOU WILL NOT FAIL, AND YOU WILL

DEVELOP CHARACTER TRAITS THAT GLORIFY GOD.

You may feel like a failure, but I want you to understand and grasp the biblical truth that in God, you can become mighty.

Be faithful and sincere in your relationship with God, for God rewards those who seek Him. Hebrews 11:6.

You can receive more from God by believing in him for one minute than by crying out to him an entire night.

It is important that you read the Word of God regularly.

Consume the Word of God until it consumes you.

Believe the Word of God in its entirety because it is the Word of God.

Always do as the Word of God says. Do not argue with the Word of God. God knows what He is doing.

The Word of God is all-encompassing, final, reliable, and eternally applicable. Your attitude toward God and His Word must always be complete obedience.

Learn to see the issues of life through the lens of the Word of God.

When Goliath went against Israel, the soldiers thought, "He is so great and mighty that we can never defeat him."

The little shepherd boy David saw the very same Goliath, the giant, and thought, "He's so big. I can't miss."

IF YOU FOLLOW THESE INSTRUCTIONS, YOU CANNOT MISS.

GOD WANTS YOU TO SUCCEED IN EVERYTHING YOU DO.

Help make a difference

Every single day New Life Outreach (NLO) makes a difference in Tanzania – one of the worlds poorest countries.

For more than 40 years, the NLO has been instrumental in shaping civil society, both socially and spiritually.

- NLO educates church planters at the Bible school.
- NLO holds evangelical campaigns in village areas.
- NLO has a girls' home for 25 vulnerable and orphans girls.
- NLO runs school for approx. 900 children. At the age of 3-17 years.

Help make a difference

- NLO provides education to more than 300 children via sponsorships.
- NLO tells children & young people about Christianity.

You can give your financial support for the work of Hannah and Egon Falk by clicking on this donate button:

Or scan this QR-code:

Support Hannah & Egon Falk QR-code

Help make a difference

If you prefer using a check, then your financial support for the work of Hannah and Egon Falk can be sent to:

LIFE UNITED
P.O. Box 18862
Shreveport LA. 71138
Phone: 318 688 4411

Please make checks out to Life United, include a note saying it goes towards Egon Falk's ministry.

Find out more about Hannah and Egon's work on:
WWW.EGONFALKMINISTRIES.COM

About the Author

Dr. Egon Falk was born and raised in a fisherman's family on Bornholm, a small island in Denmark located in the Baltic Sea.

As a young teenager during his education to become engineer he formed a Christian band and ministered all over the island.

In the year of 1969 Dr. Egon Falk went into fulltime ministry as a traveling evangelist. In 1970 he expanded his ministry and moved to Norway. 1974 Dr. Egon Falk and his wife Hannah responded to Gods call upon their lives to move to Tanzania, East Africa and began their mission work. They arrived with two small kids and a few belongings and one year later their third child was born in a small African village.

From a very small and humble beginning the ministry New Life Outreach founded by Dr. Egon and his wife with more than 100 local co-workers is now a well-known ministry all over Tanzania and even outside its borders.

The name of Dr. Egon has become a household name and even this name is not African many children are named Egon.

Dr. Egon and Hannah Falk has dedicated their lives to this great nation of Africa – TANZANIA.

Connect with Egon online:

- Author webpage: http://www.egonfalkministries.com
- Facebook: https://www.facebook.com/egon.falk
- Instagram: https://www.instagram.com/egonfalk/
- Linkedin: https://www.linkedin.com/in/egon-falk-54760a11b/
- YouTube: https://youtu.be/b-r58R-6XHw

- facebook.com/egon.falk
- instagram.com/egonfalk
- linkedin.com/in/egon-falk-54760a11b